UNDERSTANDING BRAIN DISEASES AND DISORDERS ™

PHOBIAS

ELAINE S. CHONG
AND
ERIN HOVANEC

ROSEN
PUBLISHING®

New York

Published in 2012 by The Rosen Publishing Group, Inc.
29 East 21st Street, New York, NY 10010

Library of Congress Cataloging-in-Publication Data

Chong, Elaine S.
Phobias/Elaine S. Chong and Erin Hovanec.—1st ed.
    p. cm.—(Understanding brain diseases and disorders)
Includes bibliographical references and index.
ISBN 978-1-4488-5541-4 (library binding)
1. Phobias—Juvenile literature. I. Hovanec, Erin M. II. Title.
RC535.C46 2012
616.85'225—dc23

2011019965

Manufactured in China

CPSIA Compliance Information: Batch #W12YA: For further information, contact Rosen Publishing, New York, New York, at
1-800-237-9932.

CONTENTS

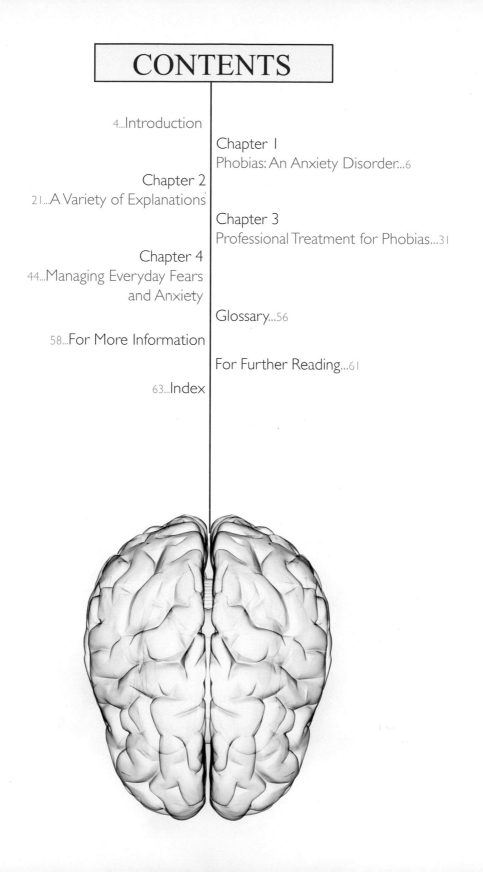

Introduction

What do you fear most, more than anything else? Perhaps you hate spiders, or you don't like heights. Maybe the thought of giving a class presentation makes you nervous. Everyone is afraid of something. Many people feel the same way that you do. These fears are all normal.

But what if spiders scared you so much that you would not walk outside your home? What if you were so terrified of heights that you refused to even look out of your second-story bedroom window? Would you fail a class if it meant not having to give an oral report? Some people would. For them, the fear is just too intense. People who have a specific powerful fear suffer from a phobia. Many phobias have an onset during the teen years.

A phobia can make a person feel helpless. The good news is that all phobias are treatable. Depending on the intensity of

At the Willis Tower in Chicago, visitors stand on a glass balcony built 1,353 feet (412.4 meters) above the ground. While many tourists seek this kind of view, people with acrophobia, or fear of heights, avoid it.

a phobia, people can sometimes manage and even overcome it on their own. In other cases, they need to seek professional treatment to deal with their phobias.

Whether you have a phobia or not, there are ways to manage fear, stress, and anxiety in your daily life. Everyone feels stressed occasionally, but you can do things to lessen the amount of tension you feel.

1 PHOBIAS: AN ANXIETY DISORDER

Everyone is afraid of something, and people fear all sorts of things. You may think that bungee jumping is a huge rush, whereas your best friend may be terrified of heights. Perhaps your mother or father loves to fish, sail, or swim, but the thought of being near the open sea fills you with dread. It is natural to be afraid of certain things, but when that fear becomes overwhelming, it can turn into a phobia.

A phobia is an intense fear of a specific object, situation, or activity. Mental health professionals have identified hundreds of phobias. Phobias come in three main categories. A specific phobia is a fear of one object, situation, or activity, such as germs, an airplane flight, or insects. A social phobia is a fear of being embarrassed in public while engaging in activities such as speaking, eating, or writing. Agoraphobia, which is a form of panic disorder, is a fear of open, public spaces such as shopping centers and playing fields.

Anxiety Disorders

Phobias are one of a group of mental illnesses called anxiety disorders. To better understand phobias and how to treat them, it is helpful to get a better understanding of anxiety disorders in general.

Anxiety disorders are fairly common. In fact, they are the most common group of mental illnesses in the United States. According to the National Institute of Mental Health

A phobia is an extreme, irrational fear in response to something specific, such as spiders.

(NIMH), about 18.1 percent of the adult population in the United States—or about forty million adults—will suffer from an anxiety disorder during a given year. Severe cases will occur in about 4.1 percent of the adult population during that time period.

In addition, according to the NIMH, a large, national survey showed that about 8 percent of teens ages thirteen to eighteen have an anxiety disorder. Females develop anxiety disorders more often than males.

Phobias are just one type of anxiety disorder. There are many types of anxiety disorders. Aside from specific phobias, some of the other major disorders are generalized anxiety disorder, obsessive-compulsive disorder, and panic disorder.

What Is Anxiety?

Anxiety is a feeling of fear, dread, or worry that often seems to have no cause. Anxiety is very different from actual fear or worry. Real, or reasonable, fear is a response to a danger or a threat. For example, if you were hiking in the woods and stumbled upon a bear, you'd likely be afraid. That fear would be real because it would have a recognizable cause—the bear—and it would be a response to an actual danger.

Real worry is a response to a troubling, upsetting, or dangerous situation. For example, you may worry that you will fail an upcoming chemistry exam at school. That worry is justifiable because it has a cause—it is possible that you may not pass the test—and it is a response to the possibility of an upsetting situation.

Anxiety, on the other hand, often does not have a recognizable cause. For the person who has a generalized anxiety disorder, he or she may feel anxious but not know why. It is natural to experience some anxiety in daily life. However, some people feel intense, persistent anxiety that is out of proportion to their situation. A person wracked by anxiety might also experience physical symptoms of anxiety, such as insomnia, loss of appetite, chills, dizziness, fatigue, tightness in the chest, hot flashes, and other ailments. These symptoms might mean that a person suffers from an anxiety disorder.

Generalized Anxiety Disorder

People with generalized anxiety disorder (GAD) can never seem to shake their persistent feelings of fear and worry. They always feel anxious and afraid, even though things may be going well. Psychiatrists (doctors who treat patients with mental illnesses) and psychologists (experts in understanding the relationship between the mind and behavior) often describe generalized anxiety disorder as "free-floating" anxiety. GAD can make a person feel constantly tired, tense, and irritable, and it can make it hard for a person to get along with others. Constant worrying can cause physical problems, too, such as headaches, sweating, muscle tension, and twitching.

Unlike people with specific phobias, most people with GAD do not avoid a certain object or situation. However, a person with severe GAD can have serious problems dealing with the stresses of daily life. To be considered GAD, the person's

People with OCD perform repetitive actions or rituals to deal with anxiety. For example, they may feel compelled to wash their hands repeatedly or to count stairs.

anxiety must last for at least six months. The disorder most often begins in childhood or the teenage years.

Obsessive-Compulsive Disorder

People suffering from obsessive-compulsive disorder (OCD) often think that, by acting out a compulsion, they can prevent some terrible event from occurring. Obsessive-compulsive disorder has two components: obsession and compulsion.

An obsession is a persistent thought that a person cannot suppress. An obsessed person may realize that the obsession is irrational or horrible, but he or she cannot stop thinking about it. A common obsession is to imagine that a loved one is going to die.

Compulsions are actions that someone does again and again, sometimes hundreds of times. That action does not seem to have much purpose. A common compulsion is to repeatedly count certain objects, anything from the steps of a staircase to the people who pass by on the street.

An obsessive-compulsive person may worry that his or her father is going to die. By repeatedly walking up and down the stairs at home and counting the steps, the person may feel that it will somehow keep his or her father safe. Of course, this is not true, and the person probably knows that. Still, a person with OCD cannot stop the obsessive thoughts or compulsive actions. Over time, these actions can start to control a person's life. According to NIMH, approximately one-third of cases of adult OCD begin in childhood.

Panic Disorder

A panic attack is a sudden feeling of powerful fear, even terror. An attack usually lasts five to ten minutes, but some of the symptoms can last much longer. Symptoms of a panic attack include trembling, dizziness, sweating, nausea, shortness of breath, and increased heart rate. People experiencing a panic attack may at first think they are having a heart attack or that they are going to die. Panic attacks can be terrifying.

Many people experience a panic attack during their life-time. This does not mean that they will develop panic disorder. Panic disorder develops when someone has repeated, severe attacks. The person can come to fear having an attack so much

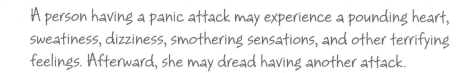

A person having a panic attack may experience a pounding heart, sweatiness, dizziness, smothering sensations, and other terrifying feelings. Afterward, she may dread having another attack.

that he or she starts to limit his or her activities. For example, people with panic disorder may be afraid to be in large crowds because they worry that they will have a panic attack and will not be able to get help. As a result, they may refuse to go to events such as school dances, sporting events, and assemblies.

Most cases of panic disorder begin between late adolescence and the mid-thirties. According to the National Institutes of Health (NIH), the disorder is twice as common in women as in men.

Agoraphobia

The lives of some people with panic disorder can become very restricted. In some cases, panic sufferers cannot do normal activities, such as shopping, without the help of a person they trust. Or, they may become so fearful that they cannot leave the house at all. When the condition gets this severe, it is called agoraphobia, or fear of open, public spaces.

People with agoraphobia fear that they may have a panic attack or start to feel trapped and anxious while out in public. If so, escape from these public situations might be difficult or embarrassing, and they would not be able to get away if they needed to do so. In a sense, people with this disorder develop a phobia of their own panic.

As agoraphobia worsens, a person will avoid social situations more and more. Eventually, the fear can become so paralyzing that he or she is afraid to leave the house. Others may

Agoraphobia, or fear of open, public places, can interfere greatly with everyday life, especially if left untreated. People start to limit their world to places where they feel safe.

not understand this fear and may not realize that their friend or loved one needs help.

Like other forms of panic disorder, agoraphobia often strikes a person in the late teens or early adulthood, and it is more common in women than in men. Agoraphobia can cause a great deal of suffering if left untreated, as it can affect every aspect of a person's existence. However, it is also one of the most treatable anxiety disorders: the condition often improves with appropriate therapy and/or medication.

Social Phobia

Social phobia—also known as social anxiety disorder—is a powerful fear of being embarrassed or humiliated in front of other people. For some people, the social phobia is limited to one situation, such as public speaking, attending a party, using a public restroom, or talking to an authority figure such as a teacher. However, in other cases, sufferers may feel anxiety around everyone other than family members.

People with social phobia often feel as though they are not as skilled or talented as other people. They may believe that every small mistake they make is a terrible error. When they do something embarrassing or attention-getting, they often feel as though everyone in the room is staring at them, even when they aren't.

As with other anxiety disorders, a person with social phobia knows his or her fear doesn't make sense but can't control it. The fear and anxiety are so powerful that the feared social activity, or even the thought of the activity, can cause a panic attack. A common way for a person with social phobia to cope with the fear is to avoid the situations that cause it.

Social phobia is not the same as shyness. There is a big difference in the intensity of the person's feelings. Shy people may feel anxious about the same things as phobic people, but they don't feel paralyzed and terrified. They may not enjoy going to

With social phobia, a person feels overwhelmingly self-conscious in normal social situations. The disorder can make it difficult to make and keep friends.

parties or speaking in public, but they don't completely rearrange their life to avoid those things. A shy person may feel self-conscious making a class presentation or playing a sport. A person with a social phobia would drop the class to avoid the presentation or quit the team to avoid being watched by spectators. Weeks and even months before the presentation or the big game, the phobic person would already be worried and afraid. Finally, a person with social phobia always has difficulty dealing with social situations, whereas a shy person is able to feel comfortable in some settings.

Specific Phobias

Specific phobias are a bit different from other types of anxiety disorders. A phobia is an intense fear that is limited to a specific object, situation, or activity. A person may have an intense, paralyzing fear of spiders but not have a fear of any other animal or insect.

There are hundreds of different types of phobias. A person may fear anything from spiders to strangers, public places to public speaking, cats to closed spaces. Some common specific phobias are fears of flying, driving on the highway, escalators, elevators, dogs, and blood.

For someone with a specific phobia of flying, the idea of sitting inside an airplane can bring on severe anxiety or panic.

People with a specific phobia feel intense, irrational fear. They may feel this way even when they are not in the presence of the feared object. For example, someone who is terrified to fly does not have to be on an airplane to feel afraid. Simply being at an airport or just thinking about being on a plane can

What's in a Name?
Thirty Interesting Phobias

The word "phobia" comes from the Greek word *phobos*, meaning "fear." An enormous number of specific phobias exist. The following list contains the names of thirty specific phobias and their triggers. Some of the names, such as claustrophobia, may be familiar to you. Others, like siderodromophobia, are probably unfamiliar.

- Acarophobia—fear of itching
- Acrophobia—fear of heights
- Alektorophobia—fear of chickens
- Anthophobia—fear of flowers
- Anthropophobia—fear of human beings
- Aviophobia—fear of flying
- Carnophobia—fear of meat
- Chaetophobia—fear of hair
- Chionophobia—fear of snow
- Claustrophobia—fear of enclosed spaces
- Cynophobia—fear of dogs
- Demonophobia—fear of demons
- Doraphobia—fear of fur
- Ecclesiaphobia—fear of churches
- Eisoptrophobia—fear of mirrors
- Frigophobia—fear of being cold
- Graphophobia—fear of writing

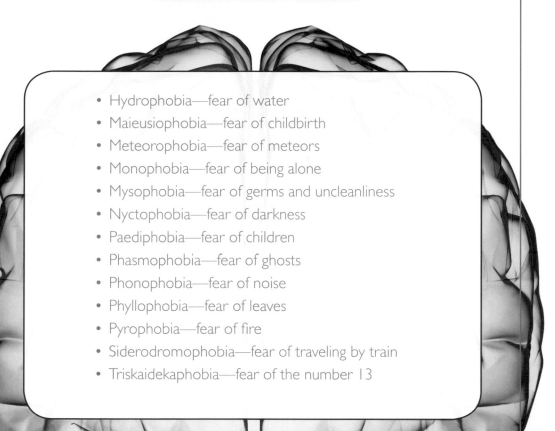

- Hydrophobia—fear of water
- Maieusiophobia—fear of childbirth
- Meteorophobia—fear of meteors
- Monophobia—fear of being alone
- Mysophobia—fear of germs and uncleanliness
- Nyctophobia—fear of darkness
- Paediphobia—fear of children
- Phasmophobia—fear of ghosts
- Phonophobia—fear of noise
- Phyllophobia—fear of leaves
- Pyrophobia—fear of fire
- Siderodromophobia—fear of traveling by train
- Triskaidekaphobia—fear of the number 13

trigger terror. As a result, he or she will probably refuse to fly and will even miss out on things like vacations and visits with family and friends. A phobic person feels powerless in the face of the fear.

Someone with a phobia realizes that his or her fear is irrational. This means that it does not make sense and that it is out of proportion to the situation. Still, a person with a phobia is unable to control it. As time goes on, he or she will probably begin to restrict his or her activities to avoid the feared object or situation. The knowledge that the fear is irrational and excessive only makes the phobia more frustrating.

Phobias are one of the most common anxiety disorders. According to the NIMH, during a given year about 8.7 percent of the U.S. adult population suffers from a specific phobia. Severe cases occur in about 1.9 percent of the adult population. Specific phobias usually appear during the teen years or in early adulthood, but they can originate in children as young as seven. Natural environment phobias (e.g., fear of storms), animal phobias (e.g., fear of dogs), and blood/injury phobias commonly originate in young children. Situational phobias (e.g., fear of closed spaces) often originate toward the end of childhood or in early adulthood. Girls and women are slightly more prone to specific phobias than boys and men are.

2 A VARIETY OF EXPLANATIONS

Believe it or not, a fear of injections, a fear of public speaking, and a fear of snakes—as different as they appear—may have similar causes and work in similar ways. Although the feared object, activity, or situation may change from one person to another, the underlying causes of the fear may be related.

Scientists do not have a complete understanding of what causes phobias. Experts in a variety of fields, such as psychology, psychiatry, and neuroscience, have proposed a number of theories. Health researchers are also investigating the impact of environmental factors, such as pollution, stress, and diet. Through continuing research, each field is contributing to our understanding of how phobias work and why people may develop them.

Sigmund Freud sits at his desk in Vienna, Austria, in the 1930s. Freud believed that phobias were the result of repressed emotions and unacceptable desires.

Psychoanalysis: Phobias Express Unconscious Desires

Sigmund Freud (1856–1939) was an Austrian physician and the founder of psychoanalysis, an early school of psychology. Freud believed that phobias, like many psychological disorders, were caused by unconscious desires. Unconscious desires are the desires that are unknown even to one's own mind. Freud believed that in childhood, people are taught that some feelings, particularly aggressive and sexual ones, are wrong. As a result, a child buries these forbidden desires in his or her unconscious mind. The process of hiding these desires is called repression.

Freud believed that people are able to express unconscious desires through phobias. These desires, which they have kept hidden deep inside themselves, create anxiety and tension. That anxiety has to be released in some way. The fear, anxiety, and stress that characterize a phobia are the release of repressed desires.

Behavioral Psychology: Phobias Are Learned Behavior

More recently, behavioral psychology has asserted that human behavior is a direct result of a person's interaction and experience with his or her environment. Many behavioral psychologists believe that phobias are behaviors that have been learned over time. A person learns to be afraid of an object or event because he or she connects feelings of fear, anxiety, and tension with that object or event.

There are two steps to this process, which behavioral psychologists call conditioning by association and conditioning by avoidance. In conditioning by association, people learn to feel fear because they associate it with a specific event. Usually, the process begins with one particularly stressful event. For example, imagine that you are swimming at a nearby lake one day and a strong current begins to swirl around you. Suddenly, you feel it begin to pull you under the water. Your heart races, you gasp for air, and terror and panic flood through you. You manage to swim away from the current and reach the shore, but your whole body is trembling, and you feel sick to your stomach. Because of this experience, your mind makes a powerful association between swimming and anxiety. It "learns" that swimming can create anxiety. In the future, swimming in the lake, or even just the suggestion of doing so, makes you feel tense and afraid.

However, conditioning by association does not create a phobia on its own. A phobia develops when you begin to avoid the object or situation that creates anxiety. In this way, a phobia develops when you "reward" yourself for behaving fearfully and avoiding something. This part of the process is known as conditioning by avoidance.

For example, by avoiding the lake and swimming, the hydrophobic person is reducing the amount of anxiety and fear in his or her life. This makes the fearful person feel better—it rewards that person. As he or she realizes that avoiding these things will make the fear go away, he or she will avoid them more often. Soon, a full-fledged phobia has developed.

Neuroscience: A New Perspective

For many years, scientists were unable to determine exactly how emotions such as fear and anxiety were related to the

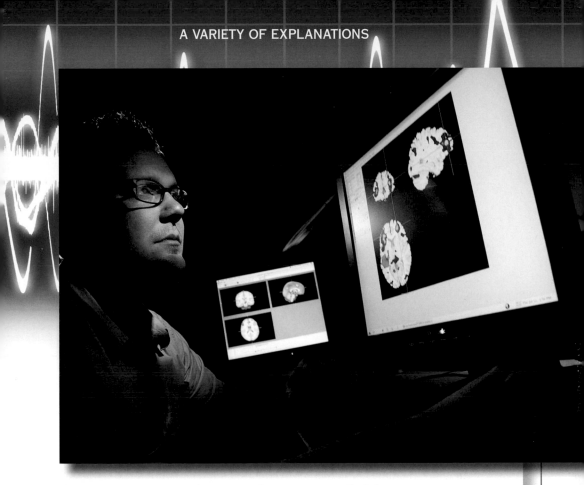

Doctoral candidate Brendan Depue views fMRI scans in the neuroscience lab at the University of Colorado. The areas in red show the parts of the brain involved in emotional memory.

functioning of the brain. With modern technology and a better understanding of how the brain works, scientists are starting to learn more about how these emotions operate in the brain.

Before modern imaging techniques were developed in order to learn about the workings of the brain, scientists observed animals and people whose brains had been damaged, or altered through surgery. They studied what happened when

25

a certain area of the brain was not working. Sometimes, they were able to dissect and study the damaged brains after their subjects died. Later, scientists used electrodes to electrically stimulate particular brain areas and then observe how the subjects reacted.

New brain-imaging techniques developed in the last forty years have given scientists powerful tools to discover how the brain functions. For example, functional magnetic resonance imaging (fMRI) is an imaging technique used by many neurobiologists today. FMRI scanners use magnetic fields and radio waves to show changes in blood flow in the brain. This allows scientists to see which areas of the brain people use most in particular tasks or situations.

Another technique used to study the functioning of the living brain is positron emission tomography (PET). This technique measures the movement of a radioactive chemical, such as radiolabeled glucose, in the brain tissue. A machine called a PET scanner detects the energy given off by the substance and converts it into three-dimensional images. Like fMRI, PET imaging helps scientists see where the brain is most active.

Fear, Anxiety, and the Brain

Using brain imaging and other techniques, scientists have been studying which brain structures are activated when people feel fear and anxiety. Researchers have determined

Built for Fear:
Key Brain Structures

Researchers have identified the following structures of the brain as important actors in the brain's fear system:

- **Thalamus.** This structure serves as a gatekeeper, receiving and passing along information from the senses to other parts of the brain.
- **Amygdala.** The amygdala scans for threats and coordinates the body's response.
- **Sensory cortex.** Part of the surface layer of gray matter of the brain, the sensory cortex processes information from the senses.
- **Hypothalamus.** The hypothalamus kicks off several of the body's defensive responses.
- **Brain stem.** The brain stem initiates certain reflexes, such as the freeze response.
- **Prefrontal cortex.** This structure is involved in processing emotions.
- **Hippocampus.** The hippocampus is involved in memory formation.

that the amygdala is a key structure in the production of fear and anxiety. The thalamus, hypothalamus, prefrontal cortex, hippocampus, and brain stem also play important roles in the brain's fear system.

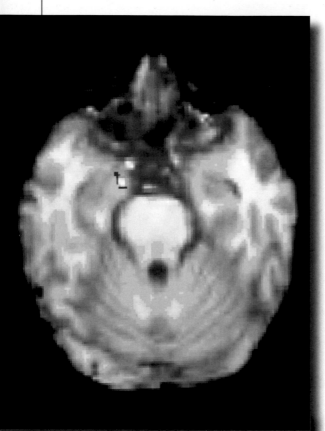

This PET scan shows the human brain's response to fear. The active region of the brain, shown in yellow and red, is the left amygdala.

The amygdala is an almond-shaped structure that is located deep in the brain at the tip of the hippocampus. It serves as the brain's threat center. Researchers believe that some of the incoming information from our sensory organs travels almost instantly from the thalamus to the amygdala, which scans the information for threats. If danger is detected, the amygdala alerts the rest of the brain and triggers a full-body fear or anxiety response. The amygdala's "alarm system" signals the brain stem to activate the body's freeze response. It also signals the hypothalamus to flood the body with hormones, such as adrenaline, raising heart rate and blood pressure and causing rapid breathing and sweating.

In addition, scientists believe the amygdala works together with the hippocampus, prefrontal cortex, and other brain areas

MYTHS AND FACTS

Myth: Phobias are a part of a person's personality. Someone
who suffers from a phobia will always have that phobia.

Fact: All phobias can be treated and cured with medication,
psychological treatment, or a combination of the two. A
person can also learn effective coping skills to reduce the
anxiety caused by a phobia.

Myth: I am the only person who has ever been afraid of snow.

Fact: In any given year, 8.7 percent of American adults have
phobias, according to the NIMH. Even though you may
think you are the only one who has ever had an irrational
fear, there are many more people out there just like you.

Myth: I don't need to treat my phobia. It will go away
eventually.

Fact: Most phobias that go on past childhood will persist until
the person receives help. Phobias can lead to other problems when they are not treated, such as social isolation,
depression, and even substance abuse. However, phobias
are often easily cured with treatment.

to store and retrieve emotional memories. For this reason, according to the NIMH, the amygdala may play a role in the development of specific fears. For example, a memory of a traumatic event involving a dog may lead to a fear of dogs.

The brain's fear system—and the "fight or flight" response that it sets off—is helpful in protecting people from real threats. However, in people with phobias and other anxiety disorders, there is runaway activity in the brain's fear system. The fear alarm keeps going off, and it is difficult to stop, even though there is no real danger. As scientists learn more about the brain, they may be able to develop more effective treatments for anxiety disorders.

Continuing Research

Scientists do not yet understand exactly why some people develop phobias and others do not. Phobias seem to run in families, although no one is certain why. Perhaps the tendency to develop phobias is passed on genetically from parents to children. Perhaps family members simply learn phobic behavior from one another. Environmental factors like diet, pollution, side effects from medicine, or physical and psychological stress may also play a role. Like other illnesses, mental illnesses are complex and probably result from a combination of factors. As experts continue to research phobias, they hope to be able to resolve some of the unknowns.

3 PROFESSIONAL TREATMENT FOR PHOBIAS

Some children with phobias get over them by adulthood. As they get older, the phobia simply disappears. However, children and teens whose lives are severely disrupted by a phobia, as well as adults whose phobias have persisted, need to seek treatment. If you suspect that you, a friend, or a family member has a phobia, don't be frightened. All phobias are treatable.

If you think you need professional treatment to conquer your phobia, you can ask someone to help you find it. First, it is a good idea to see a doctor for a checkup. He or she can determine whether your symptoms are due to an anxiety disorder or a physical problem. If needed, your doctor, parent, teacher, or school guidance counselor can help you find a qualified mental health professional. Psychiatrists, psychologists, and

Before prescribing treatment for a phobia, a doctor will do a careful evaluation to see whether a patient's symptoms are from an anxiety disorder or another medical problem.

other kinds of therapists are experienced in treating phobias and anxiety disorders. They have a variety of methods and tools at their disposal for treatment.

Therapy for phobias may be conducted one-on-one or with a group of people who have similar problems. In a group therapy setting, people with phobias can support and learn from one another. Group therapy also helps you see that you are not alone and that many people suffer from phobias.

Cognitive-Behavioral Therapy

Cognitive-behavioral therapy (CBT) is a method that is known to be useful in treating phobias and other anxiety disorders. This kind of therapy has two components. The "cognitive" part of the therapy helps people change the thinking patterns (cognitions) that have supported their fears. The "behavioral" aspect of the therapy focuses on changing people's behavior. In particular, it helps people change the way they respond to anxiety-provoking situations. CBT assumes that people's behavior and thinking patterns have been learned and that, consequently, they can be unlearned.

If you begin CBT, you will work out a treatment plan with your therapist. You will discuss what outcome the therapy should have and set specific goals that you will meet to reach that outcome. Your therapist will be there to support you throughout your treatment. He or she will also give you assignments to do at home. In most cases, the desired outcome will be successfully recovering from your phobia. CBT usually lasts for about twelve weeks.

Exposure Therapy

As part of CBT and other forms of behavioral therapy, many therapists use a method called exposure therapy to treat specific phobias. During this type of therapy, patients are slowly exposed to the objects and situations that are the source of their fears. By repeatedly facing their fears and learning to manage the uncomfortable feelings and thoughts that arise, people start to feel less anxiety. The patients are eventually desensitized to the feared objects or activities.

Conquering a phobia by facing it may sound like a simple solution, but it can be a challenging process. One form of exposure therapy, called desensitization, tries to make facing the phobia as stress-free as possible. Through desensitization, a person unlearns the association between fear and the phobic object or activity. By handling the object or activity in a relaxed, comfortable state and not experiencing any harm, the person begins to break its connection with anxiety.

Desensitization relies on a phobia hierarchy, or ranking. Along with a therapist, the person creates a list of images,

After going through a process of desensitization, situations that might have caused panic in the past, such as handling a spider, can become manageable.

thoughts, objects, and situations that trigger his or her fear. These items are ranked according to how much anxiety they cause. In this way, the phobia is broken down into a hierarchy of scenes of increasing intensity.

For example, a person with a phobia of spiders might create the following hierarchy to help overcome that fear:

- Looking at a picture of a spider
- Touching a picture of a spider
- Looking at a toy spider
- Touching a toy spider
- Looking at a live spider
- Touching a live spider
- Holding a live spider

Through desensitization, the person deals with only one scene at a time. Someone with this list would start with the spider-like object and gradually work through the hierarchy until he or she can hold a live spider without feeling anxiety.

Imagery Desensitization and Real-Life Desensitization

Depending on the severity of a person's phobia and his or her stage in therapy, two types of desensitization can be used—imagery desensitization and real-life desensitization.

Instructor Jeff Krieger helps a Florida woman go underwater during a class for people with aquatic phobias. The course helps build students' confidence that they will not drown.

In imagery desensitization, the person is exposed to images of the feared item through visualization, pictures, videos, etc. This method works best with the guidance of a therapist. But if your phobia is mild, you can try it on your own.

Using imagery desensitization, you imagine yourself in a phobia-related scene at a time when you are very relaxed, for example, after doing deep breathing. When you start feeling anxious, you immediately picture a peaceful, soothing scene instead. In this way, you can gradually build toward more intense situations without overwhelming yourself with fear and anxiety. The idea is to begin to break the connection between the feared item and anxiety, replacing the anxiety with peace. Here are the steps:

- Find a quiet, private, comfortable place to practice.
- Take a few deep breaths. Relax your muscles and empty your mind of thoughts and worries.
- Picture yourself feeling calm and relaxed in the first scene of your phobia hierarchy. Try to stay here for just a short time—maybe half a minute initially. As you practice desensitization more, you can increase the time. Afterward, if you feel little or no anxiety, imagine the second scene in your hierarchy.
- Try to stay in the second scene for at least a minute. If you feel anxious, leave your phobic scene and imagine a peaceful scene instead. Once you have relaxed, return to your phobic scene. Alternate between your peaceful scene and the phobic scene until the phobic scene no longer makes you feel fear or anxiety.
- Continue traveling up the hierarchy until you can imagine its highest level without anxiety.

Imagery desensitization may progress slowly. The entire process could take days, weeks, or even months, depending on the intensity of the fear. Most people practice imagery desensitization before turning to real-life desensitization.

If You Are Trying to Conquer a Phobia

The following are some tips to help you succeed in the desensitization process:

- **Go at your own pace.** The desensitization process takes time.
- **Expect to experience some discomfort.** Try to prepare yourself mentally.
- **Congratulate yourself,** even reward yourself, for small successes. Even the tiniest step forward is progress.
- **Anticipate failures and setbacks;** they are only temporary. Be ready to try again.

Real-life desensitization is a more aggressive approach in which the person actually comes face-to-face with the feared item. People often start real-life desensitization when they have reached midway or further through their hierarchy in imagery desensitization. Often, a therapist will accompany the person to the feared situation to provide support.

Effective, real-life desensitization can be difficult. It requires a strong commitment, since the person must be willing to experience uncomfortable feelings and to confront his or fear and anxiety. Not everyone is willing or able to face his or her phobic situation. However, if you can do so, you will most likely beat your phobia.

Psychoanalysis

Instead of behavioral therapy, you may decide to enter psychoanalysis. A person who practices psychoanalytic therapy is called a psychoanalyst. Psychoanalysis focuses on the unconscious and the ways in which your unconscious mind affects your behavior.

Unlike behavioral therapy, psychoanalysis focuses on the causes of a person's phobia, rather than the phobic behavior itself. A psychoanalyst will probably ask you lots of questions about your childhood. He or she is trying to discover what desires and feelings you have repressed in your unconscious mind.

Your psychoanalyst will spend a lot of time trying to bring out your unconscious desires. If you can uncover your unconscious desires, you can begin to work through your internal conflict. When you realize what conflicts you are hiding deep within you, you can start to resolve and overcome them.

Whereas behavioral therapy tries to change the behavior, psychoanalysis assumes that if you can reveal the causes of the inner conflict, the undesirable behavior will go away. Psychoanalysis is a long-term therapy. People spend months and often years in psychoanalysis. Partly for this reason, CBT is

10 GREAT QUESTIONS
TO ASK A THERAPIST

1. When is a fear considered irrational? Are my fears irrational or normal?
2. How do you treat your patients with phobias?
3. How long will treatment take?
4. Will I ever fully overcome my phobia?
5. Will my family be involved in my treatment?
6. Are there any medications that can help me overcome my phobia?
7. What is the name of the drug, what is it designed to do, and what are its side effects?
8. Are there ways for me to cope with my phobia besides medications and therapy?
9. What is hypnosis, and can it help me overcome my phobia?
10. Are there other people with phobias who could offer support and advice? How do I find them?

currently recommended over psychoanalysis for phobias and other anxiety disorders.

Hypnosis

Some people even use hypnosis or hypnotherapy to deal with their phobias. In hypnosis, a therapist helps a person attain a state of deep relaxation. During this time, the therapist encourages the person to let go of the fear. In mild phobia cases, hypnosis can be used to help an individual relax enough to deal with his or her fears. In more severe cases, hypnosis can allow a therapist to uncover the causes of the fear. The individual may not be completely aware of the fear's roots, as in the case of traumatic childhood events that remain in the subconscious. The theory is that once the cause of the fear is known and the event is examined objectively, the person will feel a greater sense of control.

Some people are able to conquer their phobias in just a few hypnosis sessions, while others may take longer. Still others do not seem to benefit from hypnosis techniques.

Medication

Finally, many people use medication to help manage their phobias. A psychiatrist may prescribe antianxiety drugs or antidepressants. In most cases, medication is combined with therapy

Clark Topjon manages his emetophobia, or fear of vomiting, by completing a list of thirteen daily tasks, including walking his dog, Lilly.

to conquer a phobia. This combination is usually a successful way to treat the disorder.

The amount of time a patient is required to take medication for a phobia depends on the individual, the medication, and the disorder. Many patients need to take medication for only a short period of time—often as little as two to three months. Others may need to take medication indefinitely, or may need to take it periodically due to recurrences of the disorder. Many patients have positive experiences with anxiety medications, but some experience negative side effects. Under a doctor's guidance, these patients cease using the drug. They often begin using another type of medication that works for them.

A last word: if you are experiencing very powerful, persistent anxiety, seek professional help. This is especially important if the anxiety has worsened since you have begun working on a phobia or if your fears are preventing you from functioning in daily life. Pay careful attention to your physical and mental health. If, at any point, you feel as though your anxiety is becoming unmanageable, ask for help. If symptoms are severe, get help immediately.

4 MANAGING EVERYDAY FEARS AND ANXIETY

As a teen, you are going through a stressful, confusing time. You are balancing school, friends, family, and many other things. You are starting to make decisions about your future. You are starting to consider what you want to do with your life and what kind of person you want to become. It is only natural to feel worried and afraid sometimes.

However, there are ways for you to control your everyday fears and anxiety. Your lifestyle and habits are closely connected to your mental health. Certain ways of thinking, acting, and even eating can help reduce the level of stress in your life. You may not be able to make all of your problems go away, but by changing the way you live, you can help yourself deal with them more effectively.

Change What You Tell Yourself

Your feelings, your mood, and your general outlook on life are determined to a great extent by what you tell yourself. When something happens to you, your mind interprets it in a certain way, and that is what determines how you feel about the event. For example, let's say that you play a musical instrument and you attend a tryout for a band. There are several other musicians trying out for the same spot in the band. After playing for the band, the band members tell you that they like what they heard and that they will call you when the tryouts are complete.

Start paying attention to what you say to yourself. Gently replace negative thoughts with more reasonable and positive statements.

All the way home, you think to yourself, "I played great, and the band really seemed to like me. They will definitely call me." This leaves you feeling confident and excited. On the other hand, imagine that you say to yourself, "They said they liked me, but I think they might have been just saying that to get rid of me. They're never going to call." These thoughts leave you feeling crushed and unhappy.

Think about it. The only difference between the two situations is your interpretation of the event. What does this mean? It means that you are largely responsible for the way you feel—and that you can change the way you feel. You just need a new, more positive outlook.

You may not realize it, but you are talking to yourself and interpreting events all the time. When you feel afraid, it is often because you have begun asking yourself "What if?" or saying to yourself "I can't." To overcome your fear and anxiety, try replacing these anxious messages with positive ones.

Visualize Success

Just as the things you tell yourself can help change your outlook on life, your imagination is also very useful in this respect. The mind is very powerful, and imagination is one of its most fascinating tools. Visualization, also called visual imagery, is the process by which you imagine certain events happening and the way in which you can successfully deal with them. Visualization can help you improve your performance, master a skill, and conquer a fear. Many successful athletes use visualization to enhance their performance.

Through visualization, you can use your imagination to help control your phobia. To manage your phobia, you can first picture yourself dealing with and conquering your fear. For example, if you are afraid to speak up in class, imagine yourself raising your hand, giving your teacher the correct answer, and perhaps even going to the front of the classroom to demonstrate the problem. Practicing this scene repeatedly in your mind helps you get used to it in a nonthreatening way; after all, it is only imaginary. It also gives you a chance to practice how you would deal with potential problems before they actually happen.

By imagining yourself confronting your phobia, you can get used to the idea of facing it in the real world.

Accept That You Can't Please Everyone

Often, people create stress in their lives without realizing it. As a teen, you are being pulled in a lot of different directions at once. It can seem impossible to make everyone happy. What if your teachers want you to do massive amounts of work, your parents want you to get straight A's, and your friends want you to cut class and hang out with them? What do you do? It may seem as though no matter what you do, you are letting someone down.

Everyone wants others to like him or her, but most people know that you just cannot please everyone all of the time. Some people, however, have a powerful need for approval. They feel as though they are not good enough. They feel the need to prove their worth to others. If they are not able to please everyone, they feel worried, tense, and anxious.

If you have an excessive need for approval, you probably aren't paying enough attention to your own needs. Chances are, you are not thinking about what you want or what you like. Rather, you are doing what others want you to do. Try to be realistic about other people's approval. How important is it, really? Ask yourself if this is a person whose opinion you respect. Why does this person's approval matter so much to you? What will happen if you do not get that person's approval? Most likely, he or she will still care about you, even if you do something that he or she does not like.

When you start to think objectively about whose approval you want and why, you will probably discover that it is not as important as you thought it was. Then you can relax in the knowledge that your decisions have the approval of the most important person in your life—you.

Just Relax!

Relaxation techniques can help you stay calm and in control of your anxiety. Relaxation is much more than lying on a sofa or soaking in a bubble bath. It is a psychological state in which both your body and your mind let go of stress and tension. People use many different techniques to relax. Here are some of the best:

- **Daydream.** Fantasize. Pick a specific scene that is very peaceful to you and focus on your scene or daydream. Nature scenes often work best.
- **Practice deep breathing.** Take slow, regular breaths. Breathe deeply from your abdomen.
- **Tense and relax your muscles, one by one.** Start at your toes, move to your feet, and work your way up through your body, muscle by muscle.

Some people also use meditation to relax. Meditation is an ancient practice that helps people get in touch with their inner selves. It minimizes the focus on the outer world and turns one's attention to the inner being. To meditate, find a quiet, private spot and sit in a comfortable position. Breathe deeply and empty your mind of thoughts. Let the outer world slip away and just be.

You can use relaxation and meditation to reduce anxiety before a stressful event, like a test, an audition, or a performance. For long-term benefits, however, it is important to practice relaxation or meditation regularly. If you do so, you will see its effects in all areas of your life.

Accept That You Can't Control Everything

Meditation and other relaxation techniques can help you stay calm.

Often, the things that people worry about are completely out of their control. Think about it—people worry constantly about the weather, the economy, or growing old. It is easy to stress about things that we cannot control, but it is also useless. There is nothing you can do to change them. The most you can do is prepare yourself and hope for the best.

Do you find yourself getting anxious over things beyond your control? If so, you can start practicing acceptance. Life is often unpredictable. Acceptance means taking things as they come or going with the flow. Having a sense of humor helps a lot. Try telling yourself that things will work out in the end, and that life usually turns out OK. After all, it usually does.

Acceptance also requires patience. Sometimes, things take a while to work themselves out. No matter how much you worry about an outcome, worrying will not change it. Instead, use the time you would normally spend worrying to get ready for the outcome—whatever it is. Better yet, spend that time working on something you actually can change, and change it for the better.

Deal with Your Emotions

Like many teens, you may have trouble coping with your emotions about your family, friends, school, and other things. However, it is important to find a healthy outlet for these emotions. Bottling up your emotions deep inside creates tension and stress. If you want to reduce the amount of anxiety in your life, you need to let those feelings out.

First, pay attention to what you are feeling. This means paying attention not only to your mind but also to your body. If you are experiencing the physical symptoms of tension, such as body aches, headaches, fingernail biting, sweaty palms, and twitching, notice when these symptoms occur. Do you get headaches after a certain class, or does the idea of going to a party make you break out in a cold sweat? Bodily clues can be the key to discovering the sources of stress in your life.

Writing in a journal when you're feeling anxious or upset can help you release negative feelings. It can also help you identify what tends to trigger your anxiety.

Recognize that your emotions are important. Don't dismiss them. If something is causing you anxiety, talk to someone about it. You can talk with a parent, teacher, guidance counselor, friend, or someone else you trust. If you are not ready to share your feelings with another person, try writing about them in a journal. Writing is an excellent way to release stress and let your emotions out. Finally, if you ever feel as though you just cannot handle your feelings, or that you have no one to talk to, you can call a crisis hotline. Specially trained counselors are always there to help you.

Take Care of Your Physical Health

In addition to your mental and emotional health, your physical health is also connected to the amount of stress in your life. By eating right and exercising, you can reduce your anxiety. Eating right means eating a balanced diet containing protein, grains, dairy products, and plenty of fresh fruits and vegetables. Don't worry about dieting to lose weight or vastly restricting your diet. Instead, try to eat in moderation—not too little and not too much of any one item. Try to stay away from caffeine, which is found in coffee, tea, chocolate, and soft drinks, as well as nicotine, which is found in cigarettes. These substances affect your body in ways that can increase your anxiety. If you eat a balanced diet, eat in moderation, and avoid caffeine and nicotine, you will keep your body healthy.

Exercise is good for your mind as well as your body. Exercise gives you time to clear your mind and focus on something other than your worries. You can work off some of your tension by getting your body moving. When you are done, you will

Regular exercise can decrease stress and increase your sense of well-being.

be calmer. Thirty minutes to an hour of exercise three times a week gives your body the workout that it needs to stay in shape. Do whatever type of exercise you like best. Jog, bike, practice martial arts, dance, or just walk at a brisk pace—they are all great forms of exercise.

Whether you are dealing with stress, anxiety, or fear, you can overcome these feelings. Use the techniques in this book to manage the daily stress and fear in your life. Phobias have one of the highest rates of recovery of all mental disorders. In therapy or on your own, you can learn to live without fear. When you are not afraid of what the future will bring, you can face it head-on.

Glossary

agoraphobia A fear of open, public places and situations.

anxiety An overwhelming sense of uneasiness and fear that disrupts normal functioning.

anxiety disorder A mental disorder in which anxiety is a central or core symptom.

associate To relate one thing to another.

cognitive-behavioral therapy (CBT) A form of therapy that attempts to change people's unhealthy behavior by changing their thinking patterns and using behavior therapy techniques.

compulsion An action that one feels obligated to perform repeatedly.

desensitization The process through which one "unlearns" the association between anxiety and a feared object, activity, or situation.

generalized anxiety disorder (GAD) An anxiety disorder in which one experiences chronic feelings of fear and worry.

irrational Senseless; unreasonable.

meditation An ancient practice in which techniques of concentration are used to relax, get in touch with one's inner self, or reach a higher level of spiritual awareness.

neuroscience The study of the brain and nervous system.

obsession A persistent thought.

obsessive-compulsive disorder (OCD) An anxiety disorder characterized by obsessions and compulsions.

panic disorder An anxiety disorder that develops when one has had repeated panic attacks or fears having an attack. As a result, the fear of an attack limits one's activity.

phobia An intense fear of an object, situation, or activity, recognized by the individual as being excessive or unreasonable.

psychiatry The branch of medicine that deals with the diagnosis and treatment of mental, emotional, and behavioral disorders.

relaxation A psychological state in which both body and mind let go of stress and tension.

social phobia An anxiety disorder characterized by an excessive fear of being embarrassed or humiliated in front of other people.

specific phobia A fear of a specific object or situation.

unconscious Unknown even to one's own mind.

visualization A technique that involves focusing on mental images in order to achieve a particular goal.

For More Information

Active Minds

2647 Connecticut Avenue NW, Suite 200

Washington, DC 20008

(202) 332-9595

Web site: http://www.activeminds.org

This organization aims to increase awareness of mental health issues among students on college campuses throughout North America. It sponsors campus-wide and national events to promote open discussion of mental health issues, and it provides information and resources on mental health.

American Psychiatric Association (APA)

1000 Wilson Boulevard, Suite 1825

Arlington, VA 22209

(888) 35-PSYCH [357-7924]

Web site: http://www.psych.org

The APA is a national society for physicians who specialize in the diagnosis, treatment, prevention, and research of mental illnesses. The organization's Web site for the public, http://www.healthyminds.org, provides information on many common mental health concerns, including warning signs of mental disorders, treatment options, and preventative measures.

Anxiety Disorders Association of America (ADAA)

8730 Georgia Avenue

Silver Spring, MD 20910

(240) 485-1001

Web site: http://www.adaa.org

This nonprofit organization promotes professional and public awareness of anxiety disorders and their impact on people's lives. It also helps people find appropriate treatment and develop self-help skills.

Canadian Mental Health Association (CMHA)

Phenix Professional Building

595 Montreal Road, Suite 303

Ottawa, ON K1K 4L2

Canada

(613) 745-7750

Web site: http://www.cmha.ca

As a nationwide, voluntary organization, the Canadian Mental Health Association promotes the mental health of all and supports the resilience and recovery of people experiencing mental illness. The CMHA accomplishes this mission through advocacy, education, research, and service.

Mental Health America (MHA)

2000 N. Beauregard Street, 6th Floor

Alexandria, VA 22311

(800) 969-6642

Web site: http://www.nmha.org

Through advocacy, education, research, and service, this organization works to improve the mental health of all Americans.

National Alliance on Mental Illness (NAMI)

3803 N. Fairfax Drive, Suite 100

Arlington, VA 22203

(703) 524-7600

Web site: http://www.nami.org

This national organization provides support, advocacy, and education on mental health issues. It sponsors the Web site http://www.strengthofus.org, a forum for online networking and support among teens and young adults.

National Institute of Mental Health (NIMH)

6001 Executive Boulevard, Room 8184, MSC 9663

Bethesda, MD 20892-9663

(301) 443-4513

Web site: http://www.nimh.nih.gov

Part of the National Institutes of Health, the mission of the NIMH is to transform the understanding and treatment of mental illnesses through research, paving the way for prevention, recovery, and cure.

Web Sites

Due to the changing nature of Internet links, Rosen Publishing has developed an online list of Web sites related to the subject of this book. This site is updated regularly. Please use this link to access the list:

http://www.rosenlinks.com/bdis/phob

For Further Reading

Ahern, Cecilia. *There's No Place Like Here*. New York, NY: Hyperion Books, 2007.

Bourne, Edmund J. *The Anxiety & Phobia Workbook*. 5th ed. Oakland, CA: New Harbinger Publications, 2010.

Brinkerhoff, Shirley. *Drug Therapy and Anxiety Disorders* (Psychiatric Disorders: Drugs and Psychology for the Mind and Body). Philadelphia, PA: Mason Crest Publishers, 2008.

Colasanti, Susane. *Waiting for You*. New York, NY: Viking, 2009.

Connolly, Sucheta, Cynthia Petty, and David Simpson. *Anxiety Disorders* (Psychological Disorders). New York, NY: Chelsea House, 2006.

De Goldi, Kate. *The 10 PM Question*. Somerville, MA: Candlewick Press, 2010.

Ford, Emily, Michael R. Liebowitz, and Linda Wasmer Andrews. *What You Must Think of Me: A Firsthand Account of One Teenager's Experience with Social Anxiety Disorder* (Adolescent Mental Health Initiative). New York, NY: Oxford University Press, 2007.

Gallo, Donald R. *What Are You Afraid Of? Stories About Phobias*. Cambridge, MA: Candlewick Press, 2006.

Hyman, Bruce M., and Cherry Pedrick. *Anxiety Disorders*. Minneapolis, MN: Twenty-First Century Books, 2006.

Levin, Judith. *Anxiety and Panic Attacks* (Teen Mental Health). New York, NY: Rosen Publishing, 2009.

MacKay, Jenny. *Phobias* (Diseases and Disorders). Farmington Hills, MI: Gale Cengage Learning, 2009.

Marcovitz, Hal. *Phobias* (Compact Research). San Diego, CA: ReferencePoint Press, 2009.

Metcalf, Tom, and Gena Metcalf. *Phobias* (Perspectives on Diseases and Disorders). Farmington Hills, MI: Greenhaven Press/Gale Cengage Learning, 2009.

Parks, Peggy J. *Anxiety Disorders* (Compact Research). San Diego, CA: ReferencePoint Press, 2011.

Spencer, Anne. *I Get Panic Attacks. Now What?* (Teen Life 411). New York, NY: Rosen Publishing, 2011.

Szabo, Ross, and Melanie Hall. *Behind Happy Faces: Taking Charge of Your Mental Health, a Guide for Young Adults.* Los Angeles, CA: Volt Press, 2007.

Tompkins, Michael A., and Katherine A. Martinez. *My Anxious Mind: A Teen's Guide to Managing Anxiety and Panic.* Washington, DC: Magination Press, 2009.

Van Duyne, Sara. *Stress and Anxiety-Related Disorders.* Berkeley Heights, NJ: Enslow Publishers, 2003.

Wyborny, Sheila. *Anxiety Disorders* (Diseases and Disorders). Detroit, MI: Lucent Books, 2009.

Index

About the Authors

Elaine S. Chong is a writer and educator in New York City.

Before Erin Hovanec became a writer and editor, she earned a degree in psychology from Cornell University. She also studied abnormal psychology at the University of Westminster in London, England.

Photo Credits

Cover, pp. 5, 7, 16, 17, 29, 34, 40, 50 Shutterstock.com; p. 10 Patti McConville/Photographer's Choice/Getty Images; p. 12 © Michael Newman/PhotoEdit; p. 14 Zara Jennings/Flickr/Getty Images; p. 22 Authenticated News/Archive Photos/Getty Images; p. 25 © The Denver Post/ZumaPress.com; p. 28 WDCN/Univ. College London/ Photo Researchers, Inc.; p. 32 UpperCut Images/Getty Images; p. 36 s70/Zuma Press/Newscom; p. 42 John Sleezer/MCT/Newscom; p. 45 Image Source/Getty Images; p. 47 George Doyle/Stockbyte/Thinkstock; p. 52 Ryan McVay/Photodisc/Thinkstock; p. 54 BananaStock/Thinkstock; cover, back cover, and interior background images and elements (nerve cells, brain waves, brains) Shutterstock.com.

Designer: Les Kanturek; Editor: Andrea Sclarow: Photo Researcher: Karen Huang